Accounting for Merchandising Operations

Steven M. Bragg

AccountingTools®

ISBN 978-1-64221-276-1

Table of Contents

i

About the Author

Steven Bragg, CPA, has been the chief financial officer or controller of four companies, as well as a consulting manager at Ernst & Young. He received a master's degree in finance from Bentley College, an MBA from Babson College, and a Bachelor's degree in Economics from the University of Maine. He has been a two-time president of the Colorado Mountain Club, and is an avid alpine skier, mountain biker, and certified master diver. Mr. Bragg resides in Centennial, Colorado. He has written more than 300 books and courses, including *New Controller Guidebook*, *GAAP Guidebook*, and *Payroll Management*.

Steven maintains the accountingtools.com web site, which contains continuing professional education courses, the Accounting Best Practices podcast, and thousands of articles on accounting subjects.

Accounting for Merchandising Operations

Introduction

Merchandising is all activities related to the provision of goods to customers through retail sales channels. Merchandising includes the acquisition and tracking of inventory, price setting, the creation and use of displays, discounts, and coupons, and the use of various marketing strategies. In this manual, we cover all aspects of the accounting related to merchandising transactions.

The Essentials of Merchandising Operations

A merchandising company buys and sells merchandise, rather than manufacturing it. When a merchandiser buys goods from a manufacturer or distributor and sells them directly to consumers, it is called a *retailer*. Alternatively, when a merchandiser buys from a manufacturer and sells to retailers, it is called a *wholesaler*. The typical retailer buys from many manufacturers and distributors, and presents these goods to customers in the best possible configuration to maximize its sales, using in-store displays, coupons, and discounts to maximize its profits.

A merchandising operation records accounting transactions within a relatively small number of categories. Merchandise sales appear on its income statement as *sales*, sometimes broken down further into different categories of goods sold. The use of several sales accounts can be useful for summarizing sales by different classifications of merchandise, so that management knows which classifications are selling the best and which are in need of additional marketing support.

In addition, a merchandiser uses the *cost of merchandise sold* as its primary expense category, rather than the cost of goods sold that manufacturers use. This is the total cost of merchandise sold during the period, and is directly associated with the merchandise sales recognized within the sale period. Finally, a merchandiser aggregates all other expenses into the *operating expenses* classification, which includes such expenses as rent, compensation, and utilities.

A merchandiser can have a relatively long *operating cycle*. This is the average period of time required to make an initial outlay of cash to acquire merchandise, sell the goods, and receive cash from customers in exchange for the goods. The reason for the potentially long operating cycle is that some goods can take an inordinately long time to sell; when goods have not moved for a long time, a merchandiser may have to sell them off at a greatly reduced price to a discounter, which then sells them through a variety of distribution channels at low prices.

The Merchandising Flow of Costs

The flow of costs within a merchandising organization is fairly simple. Any beginning inventory is added to the cost of goods purchased to arrive at the cost of goods available for sale. As goods are then sold, their related costs are removed from the cost of goods available for sale and charged to expense – specifically, the cost of merchandise sold. Any goods that are not sold by the end of the reporting period are then included in the ending inventory account, which appears in the firm's balance sheet as a current asset (since it is expected to be sold within one year).

There are two ways for a merchandiser to account for inventory, which are the perpetual inventory system and periodic inventory system.

Periodic Inventory System

The minimum inventory accounting system is the periodic system. It is impossible to devise an ending inventory valuation without having a functioning periodic inventory system in place. The system is dependent upon just two activities, which are:

- Compiling the cost of all inventory-related purchases during the reporting period; and
- Conducting a physical count of the ending inventory.

The compilation of inventory-related purchases is quite easy in any accounting system, and is only dependent upon recording targeted purchases in an inventory purchases account as the offsetting debit to each accounts payable transaction.

Since physical inventory counts are time-consuming, few merchandisers do them more than once a quarter or year. In the meantime, the inventory asset account continues to show the cost of the inventory that was recorded as of the last physical inventory count; the balance is not adjusted until there is another physical count or an ending valuation is estimated. The longer it takes to conduct a replacement physical inventory count, the longer the time period in which errors and inventory losses of various kinds can pile up undetected. As a result, there is an increasing risk of overstating ending inventory and understating the cost of merchandise sold over time. Given this problem, we recommend frequent physical inventory counts.

To operate a periodic inventory system, follow these steps:

1. Compile all inventory-related purchases during the reporting period in a separate account.
2. At the end of the period, conduct a physical count to derive the ending inventory valuation.
3. Calculate the cost of merchandise sold for the period, using the following formula:

Beginning inventory + Purchases = Cost of goods available for sale

Cost of goods available for sale – Ending inventory = Cost of merchandise sold

2

4. Complete the following entry to zero out the balance in the purchases account, adjust the inventory account to match the ending physical count, and record the cost of goods sold:

	Debit	Credit
Cost of merchandise sold	xxx	
Inventory purchases		xxx
Inventory		xxx

EXAMPLE

Shoes Unlimited has beginning inventory of $100,000, has paid $170,000 for purchases, and its physical inventory count reveals an ending inventory cost of $80,000. The calculation of its cost of merchandise sold is:

$100,000 Beginning inventory + $170,000 Purchases - $80,000 Ending inventory

= $190,000 Cost of merchandise sold

The company's controller records the following journal entry to document this calculation:

	Debit	Credit
Cost of merchandise sold	190,000	
Purchases		170,000
Inventory		20,000

The periodic inventory system is most useful for smaller merchandisers that maintain minimal amounts of inventory. For them, a physical inventory count is easy to complete, and they can estimate cost of merchandise sold figures for interim periods. However, there are several problems with the system, which are as follows:

- *Inaccuracy in the absence of a count.* The system does not yield any information about the cost of merchandise sold or ending inventory balances during interim periods when there has been no physical inventory count.
- *Subsequent catch-up adjustments.* The accounting staff must estimate the cost of merchandise sold during interim periods, which will likely result in a significant adjustment to the actual cost of merchandise whenever the company eventually completes a physical inventory count.
- *Obsolete inventory and scrap adjustments.* There is no way to adjust for obsolete inventory or scrap losses during interim periods, so there tends to be a significant (and expensive) adjustment for these issues when a physical inventory count is eventually completed.

A more up-to-date and accurate alternative to the periodic inventory system is the perpetual inventory system, which is described next.

Perpetual Inventory System

Under the perpetual inventory system, a merchandiser continually updates its inventory records to account for additions to and subtractions from inventory for such activities as received inventory items and merchandise sold from stock. Thus, a perpetual inventory system has the advantages of both providing up-to-date inventory balance information and requiring a reduced level of physical inventory counts. However, the calculated inventory levels derived by a perpetual inventory system may gradually diverge from actual inventory levels, due to unrecorded transactions or theft, so it may be necessary to periodically compare book balances to actual on-hand quantities. The following example shows how a perpetual system functions.

EXAMPLE

This example contains several journal entries used to account for transactions in a perpetual inventory system. Green Leaf Home and Garden records a purchase of $1,500 of fertilizer that are stored in inventory:

	Debit	Credit
Inventory	1,500	
Accounts payable		1,500

Green Leaf records $250 of inbound freight cost associated with the delivery of fertilizer:

	Debit	Credit
Inventory	250	
Accounts payable		250

Green Leaf records the sale of fertilizer from inventory for $2,000, for which the associated inventory cost is $800:

	Debit	Credit
Cash	2,000	
Sales		2,000
Cost of merchandise sold	800	
Inventory		800

Green Leaf records a downward inventory adjustment of $300 caused by inventory theft, and detected during an ongoing physical count:

	Debit	Credit
Inventory shrinkage expense	300	
Inventory		300

The net effect of these entries, assuming a zero beginning balance, is an ending inventory balance of $650.

The downside of using a perpetual inventory system is a massive increase in the number of inventory-related transactions that must be recorded. This burden may require the addition of clerks to record transactions, or the use of bar code scanning, portable data entry terminals, or other labor-saving devices.

Ideally, the inventory records within a perpetual inventory system should be highly accurate, so that the database can be used to promise on-hand goods to customers. For example, if a customer walks into an electronics store and wants to buy a 55" Samsung TV with wireless speaker connections, then the on-hand balance that appears on the sales clerk's computer screen should accurately state the number of these units that are in stock in the back of the store. If the on-screen balance shows an on-hand balance when there are no units in stock, then the store has just lost a sale. Given the sales importance of having accurate inventory counts, most large merchandisers use the perpetual inventory system. This is not the case with smaller merchandisers, which have smaller numbers of units in stock, and so find it more economical to employ the periodic inventory system and conduct occasional physical counts.

An added advantage of the perpetual system is that it always presents what should be the correct on-hand balance of inventory items. This means that a stock counter can print out a list of inventory items and what the system states should be on hand, and compare this list to what is actually there, investigating any differences found and making corrections to the inventory records. This is known as *cycle counting*.

Recording the Purchase of Merchandise

The purchase of merchandise is not quite so easy as it might initially appear to be. Merchandising firms must also contend with freight payments, purchase returns, purchase allowances, and purchase discounts – all of which are described in the following sub-sections.

Purchases of Merchandise

A merchandising company usually acquires goods on credit, though it is sometimes necessary to pay cash when their payment history is poor or the supplier needs money immediately. These goods are recorded in the merchandising company's accounting records when received. When goods are received, the warehouse staff records the receipt in its receiving log, or goes online and checks off the receipt against the authorizing purchase order number in the company's purchasing system. The supplier then sends an invoice to the company, which triggers the recordation of the purchase in the merchandising company's accounting records. When the invoice is received, a payables clerk matches the invoice to the authorizing purchase order (to verify that the price billed is correct) and to the receiving documentation (to verify that the quantity billed is correct). This process, which is known as *three-way matching*, is a cost control; it ensures that a business is not paying too much for the goods it receives. However three-way matching is also time-consuming, so it is usually limited to the more expensive purchases.

In those less-frequent cases where goods are purchased with cash, the event triggering recordation in the accounting records is the cash payment. Thus, there should be a receipt from the supplier, such as a cash register receipt, to document the transaction.

Freight Payments

When goods are being shipped from a supplier to the company, the parties agree upon who will be billed for the associated freight charges. When a common carrier (such as a trucking company) delivers the goods (which is the most common scenario), it issues a freight bill to either the supplier or the recipient.

Two key terms associated with freight are FOB shipping point and FOB destination. *FOB shipping point* is a contraction of the term "Free on Board Shipping Point." The term means that the buyer takes delivery of the goods being shipped to it by a supplier once the goods leave the supplier's shipping dock. Since the buyer takes ownership at the point of departure from the supplier's shipping dock, the supplier should record a sale at that point. The buyer should record an increase in its inventory at the same point, since the buyer is undertaking the risks and rewards of ownership, which occurs at the point of departure from the supplier's shipping dock. Also, under these terms, the buyer is responsible for the cost of shipping the goods to its facility. If the goods are damaged in transit, the buyer should file a claim with the insurance carrier, since the buyer has title to the goods during the period when the goods were damaged.

Realistically, it is quite difficult for the buyer to record a delivery at the shipping point, since this requires proper notification of shipment from the supplier. From a practical perspective, recognition of receipt is instead completed at the receiving dock of the buyer. Thus, a sale is recorded by the supplier when the shipment leaves the supplier's facility, and the receipt is recorded when it arrives at the buyer's facility. This means there is a difference between the legal terms of the arrangement and the typical accounting for it.

FOB destination is a contraction of the term "Free on Board Destination." The term means that the buyer takes delivery of goods being shipped to it by a supplier once the goods arrive at the buyer's receiving dock. There are four variations on the FOB destination terms, which are as follows:

- *FOB destination, freight prepaid and allowed.* The seller pays and bears the freight charges, and owns the goods while they are in transit. Title passes at the buyer's location.

- *FOB destination, freight prepaid and added.* The seller pays the freight charges, but bills them to the buyer. The seller owns the goods while they are in transit. Title passes at the buyer's location.
- *FOB destination, freight collect.* The buyer pays the freight charges at the time of receipt, though the supplier still owns the goods while they are in transit.
- *FOB destination, freight collect and allowed.* The buyer pays for the freight costs, but deducts the cost from the supplier's invoice. The seller still owns the goods while they are in transit.

Thus, the key elements of all the variations on FOB destination terms are the physical location during transit at which title changes and who pays for the freight. If goods are damaged in transit, the seller should file a claim with the insurance carrier, since the seller has title to the goods during the period when the goods were damaged.

In cases where the buyer is being billed for freight costs, these costs are considered part of the acquired goods, since the cost of inventory includes all related acquisition costs. Once the goods are sold, these costs are charged to expense through the cost of merchandise sold account.

Purchase Returns and Allowances

A merchandising company may not find that received goods are acceptable for a variety of reasons, such as damage to the received items or the goods not meeting the buyer's specifications. In these cases, the buyer can return the goods to the seller. If the purchase was made on credit, then the seller is expected to issue a credit memo to the buyer that offsets the amount of the returned goods that had been billed to the buyer. Alternatively, if the buyer paid cash for the goods, then the supplier should issue a cash refund. In either case, the transaction is known as a *purchase return.*

EXAMPLE

Shoes Unlimited returns a batch of shoes to the supplier due to bad stitching. The supplier issues a $3,000 credit memo to the company as soon as it receives the shoes. Shoes Unlimited records the following transaction to document the purchase return, which offsets the amount of the supplier's invoice and reduces the cost recorded in the inventory account:

	Debit	Credit
Accounts payable	3,000	
Inventory		3,000

When a merchandising company contacts a supplier about a purchase return, it is possible that the supplier will not want to take back the inventory. Instead, the supplier may offer a discount from the original billed price, and the buyer can keep the goods. This is known as a *purchase allowance.*

EXAMPLE

Shoes Unlimited contacts a supplier about some delivered shoes that are slightly out of speci-fication. The supplier offers to reduce its billing to the company by $500, and Shoes can keep the goods shipped to it. The corresponding entry is as follows:

	Debit	Credit
Accounts payable	500	
Inventory		500

Purchase Discounts

A supplier may offer a merchandising company a discount from the invoiced amount if it pays an invoice early. This discount is typically offered when the supplier is in need of cash, and so is willing to make such an offer in order to accelerate its inbound cash flow.

EXAMPLE

A supplier offers Green Leaf Home and Garden a 2% discount from the invoiced price if pay-ment is made within 10 days of the invoice date. Otherwise, payment is due in 30 days. This common payment option is contained within the invoicing code "2/10 net 30," which appears in the header line of its invoices.

Green Leaf has just received a $1,000 invoice from this supplier, so it pays within the 10-day discount terms, paying $980. The resulting journal entry appears next:

	Debit	Credit
Accounts payable	1,000	
Inventory		20
Cash		980

In the preceding example, the full amount of the original invoice is debited, in order to clear the invoice from the buyer's accounting records. The $20 discount reduces the cost of the associated goods.

Several of the most common early payment discount terms are noted in the fol-lowing table, along with the effective interest rate associated with each one.

Common Early Payment Discount Terms

Credit Terms	Explanation	Effective Interest Rate
1/10 net 30	Take a 1% discount if pay in 10 days, otherwise pay in 30 days	18.2%
2/10 net 30	Take a 2% discount if pay in 10 days, otherwise pay in 30 days	36.7%
1/10 net 60	Take a 1% discount if pay in 10 days, otherwise pay in 60 days	7.3%
2/10 net 60	Take a 2% discount if pay in 10 days, otherwise pay in 60 days	14.7%

If a merchandising company elects not to take advantage of a purchase discount, it simply pays the original invoice, not making any additional entry. Since the effective interest rate associated with purchase discounts tends to be quite high, not taking advantage of a purchase discount is generally not advised.

Recording the Sale of Merchandise

A merchandising company must deal with several accounting issues pertaining to the sale of inventory. In the following sub-sections, we address the accounting issues relating to revenue recognition, sales returns, sales allowances, sales discounts, and coupons.

Revenue Recognition

The basic revenue recognition rule is that revenue may be recognized by the seller only after a performance obligation has been satisfied. This is quite easy for a merchandiser, since the performance obligation typically occurs right away, when goods are delivered to the customer.

A large part of the sales made by a merchandising operation are made in cash or with a debit or credit card. In either case, there must be a business document that provides evidence of receipt. This is typically a cash register receipt. When sales are instead made on account (where the customer commits to pay later), the business document is an invoice copy. This invoice states the date, items sold, amounts sold, and any applicable sales taxes.

There are two journal entries associated with every sale of merchandise. One records the resulting sale, and the other records a reduction in inventory in the amount that was just sold. The first entry is a debit to either cash or accounts receivable (to increase the balance in either of these accounts), and a credit to the sales account (to increase the amount of sales recorded). The second entry is a debit to the cost of merchandise sold account (to increase this expense), and a credit to the inventory account (to reduce the amount of this asset on hand).

EXAMPLE

Epic Electronics sells a massive wide-screen TV with a complete surround sound audio package for $6,000 to a long-term customer. Because the customer has a proven record of paying on time, the sale is made on credit. Epic had previously acquired the TV and audio package for $5,000. The journal entries associated with this transaction are as follows:

	Debit	Credit
Accounts receivable	6,000	
Sales		6,000

	Debit	Credit
Cost of goods sold	5,000	
Inventory		5,000

Sales Returns

A sales return is merchandise that has been sent back by a buyer to the seller, usually for one of the following reasons:

- Excess quantity shipped
- Excess quantity ordered
- Defective goods
- Goods shipped too late
- Product specifications are incorrect
- Wrong items shipped

The merchandising company records this return as a debit to a sales returns account and a credit to the accounts receivable or cash account. The total amount of sales returns in this account is then deducted from the reported amount of gross sales in the reporting period, which yields a net sales figure. The sales returns account is a *contra revenue* account, which means that it is paired with and offsets the sales account.

Note: It is possible that a sales return will not be authorized until a later period than the one in which the original sale transaction was completed. If so, there will be an excessive amount of revenue recognized in the original reporting period, with the offsetting sales reduction appearing in a later reporting period. This overstates profits in the first period and understates profits in the later period.

EXAMPLE

Arrow Sports sells a wall-mounted basketball hoop and backboard to a customer for $1,500. A few weeks later, the customer returns the equipment on the grounds that it is broken. Arrow pays a full refund on the spot, resulting in the following entry:

	Debit	Credit
Sales returns	1,500	
Cash		1,500

There is no related inventory entry, since the returned product cannot be resold, and so is scrapped.

In the preceding example, if the basketball hoop and backboard had some resale value, then an additional entry would record the fair value of the returned items as a debit to inventory and a credit to the cost of goods sold.

Sales Allowances

A sales allowance is a reduction in the price charged by a merchandising company, due to a problem with the goods sold, such as a quality problem, a short shipment, or an incorrect price. Thus, the sales allowance is created after the initial billing to the buyer, but before the buyer pays the seller. The sales allowance is recorded as a deduction from gross sales, and is incorporated into the net sales figure in the income statement. As was the case with sales returns, the sales allowances account is a contra revenue account, so it is paired with and offsets the sales account.

EXAMPLE

K2 Outfitters sells crampons on credit to a Himalayan expedition that are slightly out of specification. The original billing was for $2,000, and the company convinces the expedition's buyer to pay for the out-of-spec goods with a sales allowance of $500. The resulting journal entry recorded by K2's accountant is as follows:

	Debit	Credit
Sales allowances	500	
Accounts receivable		500

Since no inventory is being returned, there is no corresponding inventory journal entry associated with this transaction.

> **Note:** It is important to record sales returns and allowances in separate accounts, so that management can gain a better understanding of how much these transactions are costing the company. For that reason, they should not simply be recorded as deductions within the main sales account.

Sales Discounts

A sales discount is a reduction in the price of a product that is offered by a seller, in exchange for early payment by the buyer. This is the same arrangement as was noted earlier for purchase discounts, except that now a merchandising company is offering the deal to its customers. As was the case with sales returns and sales allowances, the sales discounts account is a contra revenue account, so it is paired with and offsets the sales account.

EXAMPLE

K2 Outfitters sells a complete set of expedition equipment to an expedition that will attempt to climb an unnamed peak in Antarctica. The total invoiced amount of this sale is $100,000. K2 offers a 2% discount if the expedition can pay the full amount of the invoice within 10 days of the invoice date, which it promptly does (being sponsored by an energy drink company has its advantages). K2's entry to record this transaction is as follows:

	Debit	Credit
Cash	98,000	
Sales discounts	2,000	
Accounts receivable		100,000

Coupons

A coupon is a voucher that entitles its holder to a discount on a product. Some merchandising companies issue large volumes of coupons in order to entice customers into their stores. A coupon that discounts the list price of a product at the time of purchase is recorded as a reduction in revenue. For example, if a 20% off coupon is submitted on a $20 purchase, the amount of revenue recorded is $16.

In cases where a coupon is issued at the time of sale for the *next* purchase (as frequently happens at the grocery store), the full amount of revenue for the current purchase is recorded, since the coupon only reduces revenue if the customer elects to use it for another purchase at some point in the future. Until this coupon is actually used to reduce a list price, it is not accounted for on the books of the seller.

Accounting for Gift Cards

Many merchandising companies sell gift cards, which are purchased in specific dollar totals and then submitted when actual purchases are made. These are quite beneficial to the seller, which gains an immediate cash inflow, new customers (depending on the card recipient), and upspending (where card recipients spend more than the amount stored on the card).

There are several accounting issues related to gift cards, which are as follows:

- *Liability recognition.* The initial sale of a gift card triggers the recordation of a liability, not a sale. This is a debit to cash and a credit to the deferred revenue – gift cards account.
- *Sale recognition.* When a gift card is used, the initial liability is shifted into a sale transaction.
- *Use fees.* Some states allow a company to charge a small use fee to the holders of gift cards, which allows them to gradually reduce card balances and shift these funds into recognized revenue.
- *Escheatment.* When a gift card is not used, the funds must be remitted to the applicable state government; the company cannot retain the cash. This requirement is stated under local escheatment laws that cover unclaimed property. Consequently, there must be a system for tracking unused gift cards, which triggers a remittance once the statutory dormancy period has been exceeded.
- *Breakage.* If there is a reasonable expectation that a certain proportion of gift cards will not be used, this amount can be recognized as revenue, depending on the applicable state laws. Alternatively, these funds may need to be forwarded to the state government under its escheatment laws, as just described in the preceding bullet point.

A merchandising company should be aware of the effect of the increase in liabilities caused by gift cards. Card recipients may not use them for months, so the initial "sale" of the card only results in the recordation of a liability. This can result in a substantial liability on the balance sheet, which could negatively impact liquidity measurements. However, if there is a historical record proving that some gift card redemptions occur in more than 12 months from the current balance sheet date, a company could be justified in reclassifying the related gift card liability to the long-term liabilities classification on the balance sheet. Doing so makes the company appear to be more liquid in the short term.

EXAMPLE

K2 Outfitters sells a $100 gift card to one of its regular customers, who gives it to a friend as a birthday present. The initial recordation of the $100 cash receipt by K2 is recorded as a liability, as noted in the following entry.

	Debit	Credit
Cash	100	
Deferred revenue – gift cards		100

The recipient of the gift card uses it to pay for $95 of outdoor equipment, for which she also pays a $3 sales tax. The resulting entry is as follows:

	Debit	Credit
Deferred revenue – gift cards	98	
Sales		95
Sales tax payable		3

The remaining $2 balance on the card is unlikely to be used. K2 resides in a state where unused gift card balances must be remitted to the state government after five years have passed. At that time, the following entry is made to clear the card from K2's accounting records and forward the cash to the government:

	Debit	Credit
Deferred revenue – gift cards	2	
Cash		2

EXAMPLE

What if state law allowed K2 to charge gift card holders a $1 annual usage fee for residual card balances after one year has passed? In this case, K2 could use the following entry in each subsequent year to reduce the residual balance on the gift card, resulting in a zero balance by the end of the third year:

	Debit	Credit
Deferred revenue – gift cards	1	
Usage fee revenue		1

EXAMPLE

K2 Outfitters moves to a state that does not require unused card balances to be forwarded to the government under escheatment laws. K2 can now recognize the unused card balances as revenue under the concept of breakage. To do so, the accountant compiles a history of lapsed gift card amounts for the past few years, which yields the following information:

Percentage	Redemption Timing
65%	Redeemed within one year
14%	Redeemed in the second year
2%	Redeemed in the third year
20%	Never redeemed
100%	

It is now the end of Year 20X4. In 20X1, K2 sold $100,000 of gift cards. The preceding historical analysis has proven to be correct, with $20,000 of the gift cards purchased in 20X1 still not having been redeemed. Based on the documented history, K2 is justified in recognizing $20,000 of revenue at the end of 20X4, using the following entry:

	Debit	Credit
Deferred revenue – gift cards	20,000	
Breakage revenue		20,000

Tip: The analysis in the last example may lead one to believe that there is a fixed annual redemption rate associated with gift cards. In reality, the redemption rate is likely to increase when the economy declines, because consumers are looking for alternative sources of cash. Consequently, remeasure the redemption rate at regular intervals to see if the annual percentages are still correct.

Accounting for Warranties

Merchandising companies routinely sell warranty contracts on the products they sell, since these contracts are highly profitable. A *warranty* is a guarantee related to the performance of delivered goods. The seller typically guarantees the replacement or repair of the delivered goods.

A merchandising company does not have the operational capability to service the multitude of goods that it sells. Instead, it sells a warranty contract on behalf of a warranty servicing company, which takes on the actual warranty liability. In effect, the seller takes a commission on the sale, avoiding any further liabilities associated with the transaction.

EXAMPLE

Nile Corporation, a large online purveyor of goods, sells a one-year warranty extension contract alongside many of the goods it sells. The contracts are with General Warranty Corporation, which settles all warranty claims. Nile takes a 30% commission on all warranty contracts purchased. In the most recent period, $200,000 of warranty contracts were purchased. Since Nile acts as an agent for General Warranty, it cannot claim the $200,000 of warranty contracts as sales, but only the $60,000 commission on those contracts.

Accounting for Loss Contingencies

There may be a legal obligation for a merchandising company to compensate customers for any of its goods that cause harm. If so, this legal obligation is considered a loss contingency. A *loss contingency* arises when there is a situation for which the outcome is uncertain, and which should be resolved in the future, possibly creating a loss. For example, there may be injuries caused by a retail chain's products when it is discovered that lead-based paint has been used on toys sold by the firm.

When deciding whether to account for a loss contingency, the basic concept is to only record a loss that is probable and for which the amount of the loss can be reasonably estimated. If the best estimate of the amount of the loss is within a range, accrue whichever amount appears to be a better estimate than the other estimates in the range. If there is no "better estimate" in the range, accrue a loss for the minimum amount in the range.

If it is not possible to arrive at a reasonable estimate of the loss associated with an event, only disclose the existence of the contingency in the notes accompanying the firm's financial statements. Or, if it is not probable that a loss will be incurred, even if it is possible to estimate the amount of a loss, only disclose the circumstances of the contingency without accruing a loss.

If the conditions for recording a loss contingency are initially not met, but then *are* met during a later accounting period, the loss should be accrued in the later period. Do not make a retroactive adjustment to an earlier period to record a loss contingency.

EXAMPLE

Play Time Toys sells a variety of wooden blocks to parents for use by their children. After several years of selling an especially popular set of blocks with the alphabet inscribed on them, Play Time discovers that the supplier of this product has been using lead-based paint on the blocks. Play Time immediately recalls the product. It has no history of losses related to this issue, and so only discloses the situation in its financial statements.

In the next reporting period, several lawsuits are filed against Play Time, for which the minimum projected settlement amount is $500,000. There is no best estimate among a range of possible loss amounts, so Play Time creates a loss reserve of $500,000 against future claims.

Accounting for Sales Taxes

When a customer is charged for sales taxes, the journal entry is a debit to the accounts receivable asset for the entire amount of the invoice, a credit to the sales account for that portion of the invoice attributable to goods purchased, and a credit to the sales tax liability account for the amount of sales taxes billed.

At the end of the month (or longer, depending on the remittance arrangement with the state), the accountant fills out a sales tax remittance form that states gross sales and sales taxes and sends the government the amount of the sales tax recorded in the sales tax liability account.

EXAMPLE

International Distributors issues an invoice to Home Renovation Retailers for $1,000 of goods delivered, on which there is a seven percent sales tax. The entry is:

	Debit	Credit
Accounts receivable	1,070	
Sales		1,000
Sales tax liability		70

Following the end of the month, International Distributors remits the sales taxes withheld to the state government. The entry is:

	Debit	Credit
Sales tax liability	70	
Cash		70

Later in the following month, the customer pays the full amount of the invoice. The entry is:

	Debit	Credit
Cash	1,070	
Accounts receivable		1,070

A few states allow a business to retain a small portion of its sales tax collections as a discount. This discount is only made available if the firm remits payments on a timely basis.

Closing Adjustments

A merchandising company may need to record several adjusting entries to close its books at the end of each reporting period. An *adjusting entry* is a journal entry that alters the ending balance in a general ledger account. This adjustment is made to more closely align the reported results and financial position of a business with the requirements of an accounting framework, such as Generally Accepted Accounting Principles. There are two adjusting entries that are most commonly found in merchandising operations. They are an adjustment to the reserve for sales returns and an adjustment to the ending inventory balance. Many other adjusting entries can be found in the author's *Closing the Books* book.

If a merchandising company experiences a significant volume of sales returns, it should create a reserve for the expected amount of these returns that will be experienced in later accounting periods. This involves recording a debit in the sales returns account and a credit in the reserve for sales returns account. The sales returns account is a contra revenue account, so the amount charged is paired with and offsets sales in the current reporting period.

EXAMPLE

General Appliance sells refrigerators and other large household appliances. It has historically experienced a 2% sales return rate. In the current period, it generated $2 million of sales, so the expected amount of sales returns associated with those sales should be $40,000. It records the $40,000 in a reserve for sales returns with the following entry:

	Debit	Credit
Sales returns	40,000	
Reserve for sales returns		40,000

In the following period, General experiences actual sales returns of $39,000. It accounts for these returns with the following entry, which depletes the reserve and pays back customers for the amounts returned.

	Debit	Credit
Reserve for sales returns	39,000	
Cash		39,000

When a merchandising company is maintaining its inventory records with a perpetual inventory system, it will occasionally conduct a physical inventory count, at which point it will probably find that some adjustments must be made to its inventory records. These adjustments are usually in a downward direction, to account for losses due to theft, obsolescence, and waste. The adjustment is charged to the cost of merchandise sold account.

EXAMPLE

Utensils International runs a retail chain that sells every possible variation on kitchen utensils. It operates a perpetual inventory system. At the end of its fiscal quarter, it conducts a complete physical inventory count, and finds that the actual inventory on hand is $12,000 lower than what is stated in the firm's inventory records. It corrects its inventory book balance with the following entry:

	Debit	Credit
Cost of merchandise sold	12,000	
Inventory		12,000

Summary

There are some unique aspects to the accounting for merchandising operations, which we have pointed out in this manual. A merchandising company will likely have to deal with a variety of supplier transactions involving freight payments, purchase returns and allowances, and purchase discounts. In addition, it will probably have to account for the same types of transactions with its customers, while also accounting for coupons, gift cards, warranty contracts, loss contingencies, and sales taxes. For more detail about how to account for other types of accounting transactions than those specific to merchandising operations, see the author's *Accountants' Guidebook* book.

Glossary

A

Adjusting entry. A journal entry that alters the ending balance in a general ledger account.

B

Breakage. That amount of revenue generated from unused gift cards.

C

Contra revenue account. A deduction from the gross sales reported by a business, which results in net sales.

Cost of merchandise sold. The total cost of merchandise sold during a reporting period.

Cycle counting. The process of counting small amounts of inventory every day, comparing the results to the inventory records, and investigating any discrepancies.

E

Escheatment. A government's right to take ownership of unclaimed property.

F

FOB destination. When the buyer takes delivery of goods being shipped to it by a supplier once the goods arrive at the buyer's receiving dock.

FOB shipping point. When the buyer takes delivery of the goods being shipped to it by a supplier once the goods leave the supplier's shipping dock.

L

Loss contingency. A charge to expense for what is considered to be a probable future event, such as an adverse outcome of a lawsuit.

M

Merchandising. All activities related to the provision of goods to customers through retail sales channels.

O

Operating cycle. The average period of time required to make an initial outlay of cash to acquire merchandise, sell the goods, and receive cash from customers in exchange for the goods.

Operating expenses. All expenses associated with the selling, general and administrative functions of a business.

P

Periodic inventory system. An inventory tracking system that only updates the ending inventory balance in the general ledger when a physical inventory count is conducted.

Perpetual inventory system. An inventory tracking system that continually updates its inventory records to account for additions to and subtractions from inventory.

Purchase allowance. When a discount from the original billed price is granted to the buyer by the seller.

Purchase discount. A discount from the invoice price that is granted when the buyer pays early.

Purchase return. When the buyer of merchandise sends these goods back to the seller.

R

Retailer. A business that sells goods to the public for use or consumption, rather than for resale.

S

Sales allowance. A reduction in the price charged by a seller, due to a problem with the sold goods.

Sales discount. A reduction in the price of a product that is offered by a seller, in exchange for early payment by the buyer.

Sales return. Merchandise that has been sent back by a buyer to the seller.

T

Three-way matching. A payment verification technique for ensuring that a supplier invoice is valid, involving a comparison of the supplier invoice to the authorizing purchase order and receiving documentation.

W

Warranty. A guarantee related to the performance of delivered goods.

Wholesaler. A business that sells goods in large quantities at low prices, usually to retailers.

Index

www.ingramcontent.com/pod-product-compliance
Lightning Source LLC
Chambersburg PA
CBHW051430200326
41520CB00023B/7426